Drop by for Tea

D1520671

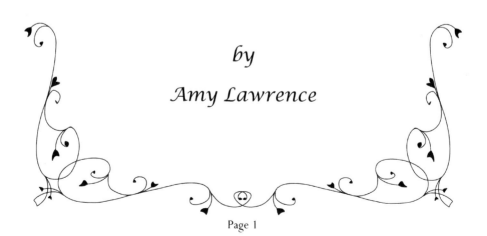

by

Amy Lawrence

Published by:

ATR Publishing

Cover Photo by:

Rob Macklin

Back Cover Photo by:

Sirlin Photographers

(916)444-8464

http://www.sirlin.com/

ISBN: 978-0-9796170-4-1

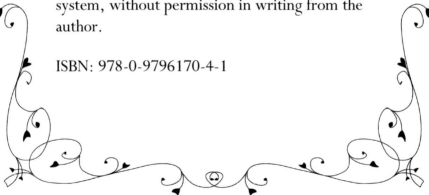

An Afternoon to Remember is dedicated to educating others in the art of taking tea. Our mission is to provide a unique upscale experience where customers are pampered and can relax, socialize and celebrate special occasions while enjoying excellent teas and delectable treats. Tea rooms entice you to sit leisurely, and this is the main goal and purpose of our tea room making your experience here truly...

"An Afternoon to Remember."

Forward

Having tea doesn't have to be a well-thought out affair. Sitting down with a nice cup of Darjeeling and nibbling on some cookies qualifies as afternoon tea. We often do not take time out in our busy lives to really enjoy the simple things. We rush around trying to get as much done as possible in a day and for what purpose really? So this year I'm really trying to focus on enjoying the moment and letting go of all the craziness at least for a little while to enjoy life and a cup of tea. Tea at my house can range from the planned event to more often than not, sitting down on the floor at least once a week with my two boys at the coffee table (should be "tea table"-huh?) and drinking from my little Chinese cups-a present from two of my wonderful staff, Ya and Yi. That's enjoying life.

So don't be overly concerned about planning the "perfect" tea party. Just make what you like, invite your good friends and enjoy each other. That's what "Drop by for Tea" is all about!

Even though my name is on the cover, this book really is a collaboration of many people. Without my kitchen staff, there would be no

Forward Continued

recipes. We sit down weekly and plan the menu and every week they come up with new and exciting recipes to share. Often times it is a twist on something they have tried but more often than not, it is something they have thought about for a while and have wanted to try and create. Carla Sherman and Dena Macklin are our chief creators. They think about every detail - the taste, the appearance, the ease of the recipe and the quality. I can't thank them enough for everything they have done for me. It's truly a miracle that they can come up with so many great ideas – especially Carla. Tea sandwich ideas are not always easy. She comes up with some very interesting and delicious recipes. This past year, Chris Jennings has taken on the salads, soups and scones. I would like to thank her especially for a great job in creating new scone recipes and tweaking some old ones. Carol Hilty has also provided great suggestions for improving our recipes.

In addition I would like to thank Arnelle Sanford, Rob Macklin and Patti Schmicking for their work on the cookbook. Arnelle is a long time customer who volunteered her time to edit

Forward Continued

all of our cookbooks and is probably cringing at
this moment as she didn't get to see this page
when editing. She is such a dear and I am so
grateful for her help. Rob is Dena's husband and
our photographer. He has taken many photos for
customers over the past year and has done two
of our cookbook covers. He really has done a
great job! Patti is my gift shop manager and chief
cheerleader. When I feel like I have no creative
bone left in my body and can't come up with a
title that conveys what I want, Patti pipes up and
says, "What about, 'Drop by for Tea', for a title
for the cookbook?" She always seems to know
what I'm thinking and what I want and more
importantly she can put it into words for me.

I can't thank my staff enough for all the hard
work they do. The tea room is really a labor of
love. It's not just about the food, it's about the
experience and these people always go the extra
mile to make sure everything happens for you.
They are always there for me whether it's Fran
who stays late for a networking event and then
take tablecloths home to wash, or Patti who is
always ready to come in at 6:00 am. to get ready
to teach class, or Ya and Yi to come in early on a

Forward Continued

Saturday to make extra scones, or Micki to take laundry home and then go to the grocery store after a long day or Ploy who will do just about anything for you at a last minute's notice. Everyone contributes in their own way. I can never tell them how much I truly appreciate and love them for all that they do. I would like to thank each and every one of them from the bottom of my heart.

I would also like to thank my family, particularly my husband, Pat. Not only does he keep me going in life, he's the reason the cookbook ever gets printed. He stays up all hours of the night meticulously going through each page and designing the cover so that it complies with the exact specifications of the publisher. He's my hero and the love of my life.

My two boys, Thomas and Jacob are also the loves of my life. They help out in every way they can and keep me smiling.

And last but not least, I would like to thank all of my wonderful and dedicated customers. You're the reason I'm still here doing what I love - making people happy!

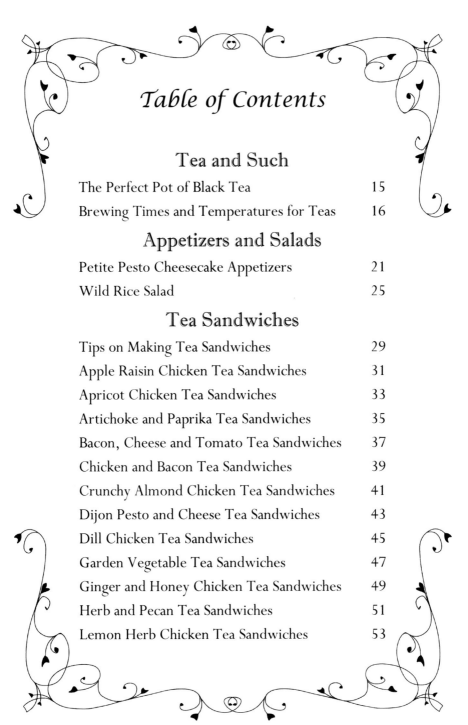

Table of Contents

Tea and Such

Appetizers and Salads

Tea Sandwiches

Table of Contents Continued

Tea Sandwiches

Desserts

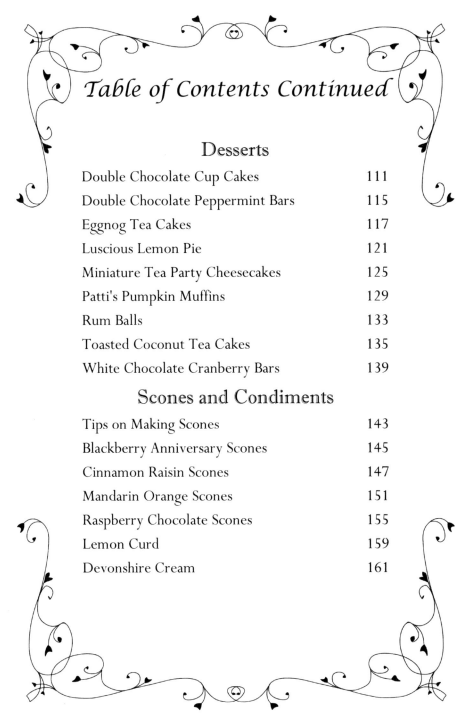

Table of Contents Continued

Desserts

Scones and Condiments

Tea and Such

The Perfect Pot of Black Tea

Fill kettle with freshly drawn cold water.

Temper teapot by filling with hot water.

Bring kettle to boil.

Pour out water in teapot.

Place tea sock in teapot.

Add one scant teaspoon of tea per cup.

Pour boiling water over leaves.

Replace teapot lid.

Steep for 3-5 minutes for black tea.

Decant or remove tea sock with leaves.

Stir and serve.

Cover with a tea cozy or use a warmer to keep tea piping hot.

Enjoy!

Brewing Teas and Tissanes

White Teas

Water – hot, about 180°
Steeping time – White teas are very mild. To get the full flavor, steep for 10-12 minutes.

Green Teas

Water – hot, about 180°
Steeping time – Most green teas can be steeped more than once. If multiple infusions are desired then start with a steeping time of 2 minutes and then increase it by 1 minute for every additional infusion.

Oolongs

Water – a little less than boiling – around 195°
Steeping time – same as green teas

Black Tea

Water – almost boiling
Steeping time – normally 3-4 minutes. Some Darjeelings are best at 3 minutes.

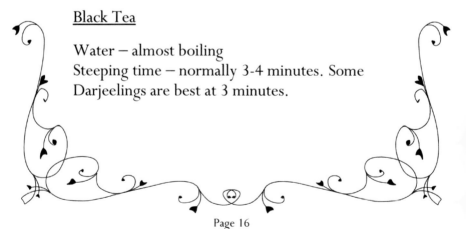

Brewing Teas and Tissanes Continued

<u>Flavored Black Teas</u>

Water – almost boiling
Steeping time – 3-4 minutes

<u>Tisanes or Herbal Blends</u>

Water – boiling

Steeping time – 7 minutes

Appetizers and Salads

Petite Pesto Cheesecake Appetizers

We like to use the mini spring form pans for this recipe. Our pans are 4½" in diameter. We cut each cheese cake into 4 wedges. You can also use a 9" spring form pan and cut it into 16 slices.

- 1 c. dry bread crumbs
- ¼ c. butter, melted
- ⅓ c. olive oil
- 2 c. fresh basil leaves
- ½ c. parsley, chopped
- ½ t. salt
- 1 garlic clove cut in half
- 2 8 oz. cream cheese, softened
- 1 c. ricotta cheese
- 3 eggs
- ½ c. grated parmesan cheese
- ½ c. pine nuts
- Basil leaves for garnish
- Cherry tomatoes sliced in half for garnish

Mix melted butter and bread crumbs together. Press into spring form pan(s). Bake at 350° for 5 minutes if using 4 mini pans or 10 minutes if using 9" pan.

Notes

Petite Pesto Cheesecake Appetizers Continued

Place oil, basil, parsley, salt and garlic in blender. Blend on high speed until smooth. Combine basil mixture, cream cheese and ricotta in a medium bowl. Blend with an electric mixer until well blended. Add eggs, one at a time, mixing well after each addition. Blend in parmesan cheese, then pour mixture over crust. Top with pine nuts. Bake at 325° 30-40 minutes for mini pans or about 95 minutes for large pan. With a knife loosen cake from rim of pan, cool before removing rim of pan. Serve warm or at room temperature. Place sliced appetizer on plate; garnish with basil leaf and slice of cherry tomato and lay on leaf.

Notes

Wild Rice Salad

- 1 can (13¾ oz.) beef broth (reserve 2 T. broth)
- 1 pkg. (6 oz.) long grain wild rice
- 1 can (11 oz.) mandarin oranges, drained or use fresh
- 1 can (8 oz.) sliced water chestnuts, drained
- ¼ c. green onions, sliced diagonally
- ⅓ c. mayonnaise
- Lettuce leaves

Reserve 2 T. broth and set aside. Add enough water to remaining broth to substitute for water called for in rice package directions (omit butter or margarine). Cook rice according to directions. Cool. Stir in oranges, water chestnuts and green onions. Blend reserved broth and mayonnaise. Add to rice mixture. Cover and refrigerate 2-3 hours. Serve on lettuce leaves or line tea cups with lettuce leaves and serve in the tea cups. Makes about 6-8 servings.

Notes

Tea Sandwiches

Tips on Making Tea Sandwiches

Make your sandwich fillings ahead of time - most can be made up to 3 days in advance.

If you are making chicken, always use fresh chicken, not canned.

If you are making a tea sandwich with cream cheese filling, always soften the cream cheese before making the filling. Add freshly chopped herbs whenever possible. If you use a little sour cream in the cream cheese mixture, it will make your filling easier to spread.

Always butter the bread before spreading on the filling, otherwise the filling will "leak" through.

Make your sandwiches the day before. Wrap well. Cut them the day of your event. The filling will be cold and solidified so they will slice nicely. If you do them the same day, it's hard to get a "clean" edge.

Use fresh herbs, or chopped veggies for garnish. If you're making an olive sandwich, slice an olive and garnish on top. Always garnish the day of the event for the best look.

Tips on Making Tea Sandwiches Continued

Extra Tips:
- Don't press down when you cut.
- Try to handle them as little as possible.

Apple Raisin Chicken Tea Sandwiches

- 2 c. cooked chicken – pulse in food processor, lightly or chop finely
- 3 T. green onions, chopped
- ½ c. apples, chopped
- ¼ c. raisins
- 1 t. dried tarragon, plus extra for decoration
- Salt and pepper to taste
- Mayo
- Bread
- Butter

Mix together first 6 ingredients. Add just enough mayonnaise to bind the mixture together. Spread butter on bread. Add filling and top with second slice. Cut into desired shapes. Sprinkle parsley or tarragon on sides of sandwiches for decoration if desired. Makes about 16 tea sandwiches.

Notes

Apricot Chicken Tea Sandwiches

- 2 c. cooked chicken – pulse in food processor, lightly or chop finely
- 3 T. green onions, chopped
- ½ c. apricot preserves
- 2 t. soy sauce
- 1 t. lemon juice
- Salt and pepper to taste
- Mayo
- Bread
- Butter
- Parsley for garnish

Mix together first 6 ingredients. Add just enough mayonnaise to bind the mixture together. Spread butter on bread. Add filling and top with second slice. Cut into desired shapes. Sprinkle parsley on sides of sandwiches for decoration if desired. Makes about 16 tea sandwiches.

Notes

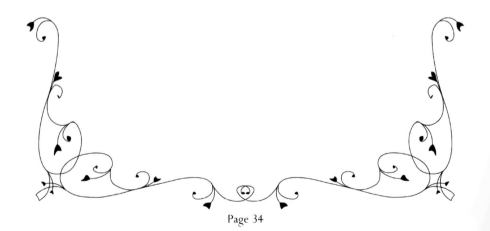

Artichoke and Paprika Tea Sandwiches

- 1 8 oz. pkg. cream cheese softened
- ½ c. sour cream
- ¼ c. grated parmesan cheese
- 1 envelope golden onion soup mix
- 9 oz. chopped artichokes – drained
- Butter
- Bread
- Artichokes for garnish
- Paprika for garnish

Beat cream cheese and sour cream together. Mix in parmesan cheese, soup mix and artichokes. Butter slices of bread. Top with spread. Cut into slices. Garnish with a small artichoke heart and sprinkle with paprika. Makes about 32 tea sandwiches.

Notes

Bacon, Cheese and Tomato Tea Sandwiches

- 1 8 oz. pkg cream cheese, softened
- ½ c. sour cream
- 4 slices cooked and crumbled bacon
- ¼ c. grated parmesan cheese
- 2 T. onion, chopped
- 1 T. fresh parsley, chopped
- Dark rye bread
- Fresh parsley for garnish
- Cherry Tomatoes cut in half for garnish

Beat cream cheese until smooth. Gradually add in sour cream. Mix in remaining ingredients. If mixture is still too hard to spread add a bit more sour cream. Butter bread slices. Spread cream cheese mixture on slice. Cut into four slices. Garnish with a cherry tomato half. Makes about 32 tea sandwiches.

Notes

Chicken Bacon Tea Sandwiches

- 2 c. cooked chicken-pulse in food processor, lightly or chop finely
- 5 strips of bacon, cooked and crumbled
- 1 8 oz. can chopped water chesnuts
- 2 stalks of celery thinly sliced
- 1 T. fresh parsley, chopped
- 3 T. green onions, chopped
- Salt and pepper to taste
- Mayo
- Bread
- Butter
- Dried

Mix together first 7 ingredients. Add just enough mayonnaise to bind the mixture together. Spread butter on bread. Add filling and top with second slice. Cut into desired shapes. Sprinkle parsley on sides of sandwiches for decoration if desired. Makes about 16 tea sandwiches.

Notes

Crunchy Almond Chicken Tea Sandwiches

- 2 c. cooked chicken — pulse in food processor, lightly or chop finely
- 3 T. green onions, chopped
- ½ c. slivered almonds, toasted
- ½ envelope Italian dressing
- ½ t. ginger
- Salt and pepper to taste
- Mayo
- Bread
- Butter
- Parsley for garnish

Mix together first 6 ingredients. Add just enough mayonnaise to bind the mixture together. Spread butter on bread. Add filling and top with second slice. Cut into desired shapes. Sprinkle parsley on sides of sandwiches for decoration if desired. Makes about 16 tea sandwiches.

Notes

Dijon Pesto and Cheese Tea Sandwiches

- 1 8 oz. pkg. cream cheese
- ½ c. sour cream
- 4 T. fresh parsley, chopped
- 2 T. Dijon mustard
- 2 T. walnuts, chopped
- 1 T. dried basil
- 1 clove garlic, chopped
- 2 T grated parmesan cheese
- Walnuts for garnish
- Butter
- Bread

Beat cream cheese until smooth. Gradually add in sour cream. Mix in remaining ingredients. Butter bread slices. Spread cream cheese mixture on slice. Cut into four squares. Garnish with a whole walnut and a bit of parmesan cheese. Makes about 32 tea sandwiches.

Notes

Dill Chicken Tea Sandwiches

- 2 c. cooked chicken-pulse in food processor, lightly or chop finely
- ½ pkg. Italian dressing
- ½ c. loosely packed fresh dill, chopped
- 3 T. green onions, chopped
- 2 T. snipped chives
- Salt and pepper to taste
- Mayo
- Dried Parsley for garnish
- Butter
- Bread, buttermilk works well

Mix together first 6 ingredients. Add just enough mayonnaise to bind the mixture together. Spread butter on bread. Add filling and top with second slice. Cut into desired shapes. Sprinkle parsley or dill on sides of sandwiches for decoration if desired. Makes about 16 tea sandwiches.

Notes

Garden Vegetable Tea Sandwiches

- 8 oz cream cheese, softened
- ½ c. shredded carrots
- ½ c. shredded zucchini
- 1 T. fresh parsley, chopped
- ½ c. water chestnuts, chopped – well drained
- Garlic salt and pepper to taste
- Bread-dark rye looks very nice
- Butter
- Shredded carrots
- Shredded zucchini

Beat cream cheese until smooth. Add carrots, zucchini, parsley, water chestnuts, garlic salt, and pepper. Butter bread slices. Spread cream cheese mixture on slice. Cut into four slices. Garnish with shredded carrots or zucchini. Makes about 32 tea sandwiches.

Notes

Ginger and Honey Chicken Tea Sandwiches

- 2 c. chicken – pulse in food processor, lightly or chop finely
- 3 T. green onions, chopped
- ½ c. picante sauce
- ⅓ c. honey
- 3 T. soy sauce
- 4 T. Dijon style mustard
- 1 T. grated fresh ginger
- ¼ t. grated orange peel
- Mayonnaise
- Salt and pepper to taste
- Parsley for decoration

Mix together first 9 ingredients. Add just enough mayonnaise to bind the mixture together. Spread butter on bread. Add filling and top with second slice. Cut into desired shapes. Sprinkle parsley on sides of sandwiches for decoration if desired. Makes about 16 tea sandwiches.

Notes

Herb and Pecan Tea Sandwiches

- 8 oz. cream cheese, softened
- ½ c. sour cream
- 2 T. fresh parsley, chopped
- 2 t. lemon juice
- 1 T. fresh basil, chopped
- ¼ c. pecans, chopped
- 1 T. Worcestershire sauce
- Butter
- Slices of bread-rye works great
- Fresh parsley for garnish
- Pecan halves for garnish

Beat cream cheese until smooth. Gradually add in sour cream. Add parsley, lemon juice, basil, pecans and Worcestershire sauce. Butter bread slices. Spread cream cheese mixture on slice. Cut into four slices. Garnish with a sprig of fresh parsley or a pecan half. Makes about 32 tea sandwiches.

Notes

Lemon Herb Chicken Tea Sandwiches

- 2 c. cooked chicken – pulse in food processor, lightly or chop finely
- 3 T. green onions, chopped
- 1 T. rosemary, chopped
- 2 T. parsley, chopped
- ¼ c. lemon juice
- ½ t. thyme, chopped
- Pepper and garlic salt to taste
- Mayo
- Bread
- Butter
- Parsley for garnish
- Grated lemon for garnish

Mix together first 7 ingredients. Add just enough mayonnaise to bind the mixture together. Spread butter on bread. Add filling and top with second slice. Cut into desired shapes. Sprinkle parsley mixed with grated lemon on sides of sandwiches for decoration if desired. Makes about 16 tea sandwiches.

Notes

Orange Tarragon Chicken Tea Sandwiches

- 2 c. cooked chicken – pulse in food processor, lightly or chop finely
- 3 T. green onions, chopped
- 1 pkg. onion mushroom soup mix
- 8 oz. orange marmalade
- ⅓ c. orange juice
- 1 t. dried tarragon
- Salt and pepper to taste
- Butter
- Bread
- Grated orange peel or dried tarragon for garnish

Mix together first 7 ingredients. Add just enough mayonnaise to bind the mixture together. Spread butter on bread. Add filling and top with second slice. Cut into desired shapes. Sprinkle grated orange peel or dried tarragon on sides of sandwiches for garnish if desired. Makes about 16 tea sandwiches.

Notes

Philly Mushroom Tea Sandwiches

- 1 8 oz. pkg. cream cheese, softened
- 2 lb. fresh mushrooms, sliced
- 2 T. onions
- 3 T. butter
- ½ c. blue cheese
- Butter
- Slices of bread – dark rye looks very nice with this spread
- Fresh parsley for garnish

Saute' mushrooms and onions together in 3 T. butter until cooked and soft. Drain well. Beat cream cheese. Mix in mushrooms mixture, and blue cheese. Butter slices of bread. Top with spread. Cut into slices. Garnish with a fresh sprig of parsley. Makes about 32 tea sandwiches.

Notes

Roasted Red Pepper with Parmesan Tea Sandwiches

- 8 oz. cream cheese, softened
- ½ c. sour cream
- 1 jar (8oz) roasted red peppers chopped, well drained
- 1 c. basil, chopped
- ¼ c. grated parmesan cheese
- 1 clove garlic, minced
- Salt and pepper to taste
- Butter
- Slices of bread-dark bread looks very nice for this filling
- Red pepper or cucumber for garnish

Beat cream cheese until smooth. Gradually add in sour cream. Mix in remaining ingredients. Butter bread slices. Spread cream cheese mixture on slice. Cut into four slices. Garnish with a slice of red pepper or a cucumber. Makes about 32 tea sandwiches.

Notes

Spanish Olive Tea Sandwiches

- 1 8 oz. cream cheese, softened
- 2 T. sour cream
- 1 can chopped chilies
- ½ c. chopped black olives
- ½ c. sweet red pepper, chopped
- 2 t. grated onion
- ¼ t. Tabasco sauce
- Butter
- Bread

Mix all ingredients together. Spread a small amount of butter on bread then spread on cream cheese mixture. Cut sandwiches into 4 squares and top with a cilantro leaf or a thin slice of red pepper. Makes about 32 tea sandwiches.

Notes

Spicy Chicken Taco Tea Sandwich

- 2 c. cooked chicken – pulse in food processor, lightly or chop finely
- 3 T. green onions, chopped
- 1 pkg. taco seasoning
- ¾ c. shredded cheddar cheese
- ½ c. cilantro, chopped
- Mayonnaise
- Salt and pepper to taste
- Butter
- Bread – buttermilk works well
- Parsley for decoration

Mix together first 6 ingredients. Add just enough mayonnaise to bind the mixture together. Spread butter on bread. Add filling and top with second slice. Cut into desired shapes. Sprinkle parsley on sides of sandwiches for decoration if desired. Makes about 16 tea sandwiches depending on thickness and size of sandwich.

Notes

Sweet and Spicy Chicken Tea Sandwiches

- 2 c. cooked chicken – pulse in food processor, lightly or chop finely
- 3 T. green onions, chopped
- ½ c. orange marmalade
- ⅓ c. teriyaki sauce
- ¼ c. brown sugar
- ¼ t. ground cloves
- ¼ t. ground ginger
- Mayonnaise
- Salt and pepper to taste
- Bread – buttermilk bread works well
- Butter

Mix together first 8 ingredients. Add just enough mayonnaise to bind the mixture together. Spread butter on bread. Add filling and top with second slice. Cut into desired shapes. Sprinkle parsley on sides of sandwiches for decoration if desired. Makes about 16 tea sandwiches depending on thickness and size of sandwich.

Notes

Swiss Cheese and Bacon Tea Sandwiches

- 2 c. shredded swiss cheese
- ½ c. sour cream
- 8 oz. cream cheese, softened
- 2 T. minced onion
- 4 slices of bacon, cooked to crisp, crumbled
- ½ t. salt
- ½ t. garlic powder
- Dark rye bread slices
- Sliced cherry tomatoes cut in half

Beat cream cheese until smooth. Add in sour cream. Mix in swiss cheese, onion, bacon, salt and garlic powder and sour cream. If mixture is too hard to spread use a bit more sour cream. Spread on lightly buttered dark rye bread. Cut as desired. Top with a slice of tomato. Sprinkle with pepper if desired. Makes about 32 tea sandwiches.

Notes

Spicy Bean on Pita

- 3 oz. cream cheese softened
- 2 T. sour cream
- 1 can refried beans
- ¼ c. salsa
- 1 clove minced garlic
- Cilantro leaves for garnish
- Black olive slices
- 1 pkg pita bread (with about 6-8 pitas in a pkg.)

Preheat oven to 350°. Cut pita in small triangles (about 8 triangles per pita). Place on a cookie sheet and toast about 15 minutes or until crisp. Mix cream cheese, sour cream, beans, salsa, garlic together. Spread bean mixture on top of pita triangle. Top with cilantro leaf or a black olive slice. Serve immediately. Makes about 32-48 depending on number of pitas in package.

Notes

Desserts

Almond Roca Brittle Bars

Base

- 1 ¾ c. butter
- 1 c. sugar
- ⅔ c. brown sugar
- 2 t. almond extract
- 2 c . semi sweeet chocolate chips
- 1 ½ c. SKOR toffee bits
- 3 c. flour
- ½ c. almonds
- 1 t. baking soda
- 1 ½ t. salt

Topping

- 2 c. semi sweet chocolate chips
- 1 T. oil
- 1 c. finely chipped almonds
- 1 c. crushed toffee bits (or crush Almond Rocca candy)

Mix all of the base ingredients with an electric mixer until well combined. Spread evenly into a well greased 9"x13" baking pan. Bake at 375° for 12-15 minutes.

Melt 2 c. semi sweet chocolate chips in the

Notes

Almond Roca Brittle Bars
Continued

microwave for 1 minute. Remove and add 1 T. oil. Stir well. Return to microwave for an additional 35 seconds or until melted. Drizzle melted chocolate mixture over the top of the brittle base. Sprinkle finely chopped almonds, toffee bits over top of melted chocolate. Refrigerate for approximately 1 hour and then cut into bars. Makes about 24 bars.

Notes

Apricot Delights

- 1 c. butter
- ½ c. sugar
- ½ c. brown sugar
- 1 egg
- 1 T. apricot jam
- 1 ½ t. pure vanilla extract
- ¼ t. baking soda
- ¼ t. salt
- 2 ½ c. flour
- ¾ c. white chocolate chips
- ¼ c. dried apricots
- ¼ c. coconut

Apricot Glaze

- 1 ¼ c. powdered sugar
- 1 t. vanilla
- 2 T. apricot jam (heat a bit before mixing it in)

Preheat oven to 400°. Cream butter, sugar and brown sugar together. Add egg, apricot jam, and vanilla. Beat at medium speed in mixer until light and fluffy. Add flour, baking soda, and salt and remaining ingredients. Beat at low speed until soft dough forms. Drop by teaspoonful and bake at 400° for 5 minutes. Cool completely and

Notes

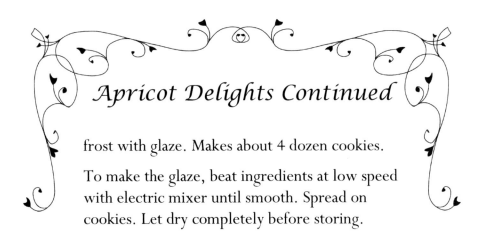

Apricot Delights Continued

frost with glaze. Makes about 4 dozen cookies.

To make the glaze, beat ingredients at low speed with electric mixer until smooth. Spread on cookies. Let dry completely before storing.

Notes

Cherry Sugar Drops

- 1 c. butter
- ½ c. sugar
- ½ c. brown sugar
- 1 egg
- 1 c. dried cherries
- ½ c. mini chocolate chips
- 2 t. cherry juice
- 1 t. vanilla extract
- ¼ t. baking soda
- ¼ t. salt
- 2 ½ c. flour

Cherry glaze:

- 1 ¼ c. powdered sugar
- 1 t. vanilla
- 4-5 T. cherry juice

Cream butter, sugar, and brown sugar together. Add egg, cherry juice, and vanilla. Beat at medium speed in a mixer until light and fluffy. Add flour, baking soda, and salt. Beat at low speed until soft dough forms. Add the dried cherries and mini chocolate chips until well combined. Drop by teaspoonful onto a cookie sheet. Bake at 375° for 6 minutes.

Notes

Cherry Sugar Drops
Continued

Cool completely. Makes about 4 dozen.

Combine glaze ingredients. Beat at low speed with electric mixer until smooth. Drizzle or dip cookies. Top with a few mini chocolate chips. Let dry completely before storing.

Notes

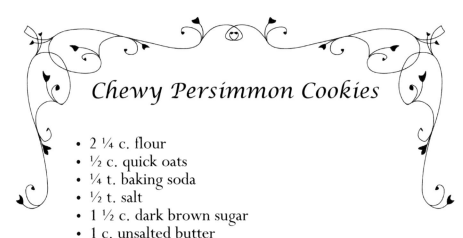

Chewy Persimmon Cookies

- 2 ¼ c. flour
- ½ c. quick oats
- ¼ t. baking soda
- ½ t. salt
- 1 ½ c. dark brown sugar
- 1 c. unsalted butter
- 2 large eggs
- 1 T. pure vanilla extract
- 1 ½ c. chopped persimmons
- 1 t. cinnamon
- 1 t. ginger
- 1 c. white chocolate chips

Glaze:

- 1 ¼ c. powdered sugar
- 2-4 T. milk
- 1 T. persimmon puree (peel a persimmon, chop into pieces, puree in food processor)
- 1 t. grated orange peel

Preheat over to 300°. (Yes, it's really 300°).

Beat butter and brown sugar well. Add eggs and vanilla and mix thoroughly. Add the dry ingredients. Mix well and then add the white

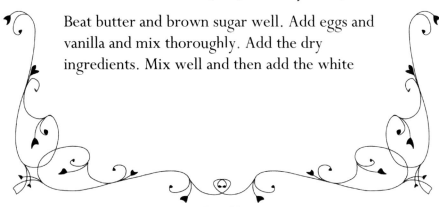

Notes

Chewy Persimmon Cookies Continued

chocolate chips and persimmons. Mix until combined. Drop by teaspoonfuls onto a cookie sheet.

Bake for 18-20 minutes. Let cool completely.

Glaze:

Mix powdered sugar, persimmon puree and orange peel together. Add enough milk to make a drizzling consistency. Drizzle over cooled cookies. Let glaze set.

Makes about 6 dozen cookies.

Notes

Chocolate Cheesecake Infusion

- 1 box chocolate cake mix
- 1 lg. box instant chocolate pudding
- 1 c. buttermilk
- 4 eggs
- ½ c. vegetable oil
- ½ c. water or ½ c. coffee
- 1 c. semisweet chocolate chips

Infusion:

- 8 oz. cream cheese, softened
- ½ c. sugar
- 2 eggs

Ganache:

- 8 oz. semisweet chocolate chips
- ¾ c. whipping cream
- 2 T. unsalted butter
- 2 T. brandy

Mix cake mix, pudding, buttermilk, 4 eggs, oil, water and together in a large mixing bowl. Mix 3 minutes on medium speed until well blended. Add chocolate chips on low speed of mixer. Set aside.

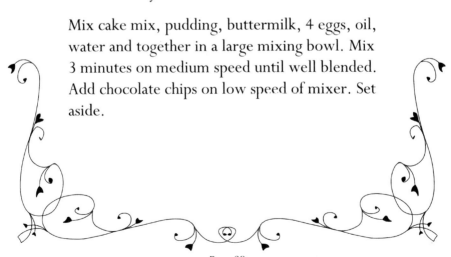

Notes

Chocolate Cheesecake Infusion Continued

In a separate mixing bowl mix cream cheese until light and fluffy. Add sugar and 2 eggs. Mix until smooth and creamy.

Spray mini bundt pans with flour spray. Using an ice cream scoop or spoon, fill the mini bundt pans ⅔ full with the chocolate batter. Fill a piping bag with the cream cheese mixture. Use a small tip on the piping bag and insert tip into center of uncooked cakes. Squeeze to put a good size dollop of mixture into the center of each cake.

Bake at 350° for 8-15 minutes until golden brown or when done when a toothpick is inserted. Cool completely.

Ganache:

Place chocolate chips, whipping cream and butter into a bowl. Microwave for about 1 ½ minutes. Using a wire whisk beat chocolate. Add 2 T. brandy and whisk until shiny and smooth. If chocolate isn't melted enough, melt for another

Notes

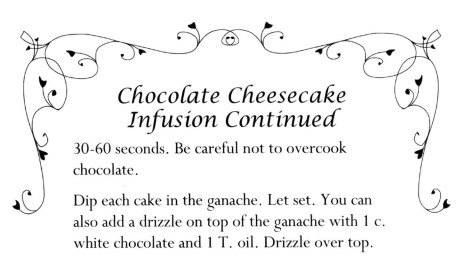

Chocolate Cheesecake
Infusion Continued

30-60 seconds. Be careful not to overcook chocolate.

Dip each cake in the ganache. Let set. You can also add a drizzle on top of the ganache with 1 c. white chocolate and 1 T. oil. Drizzle over top.

Makes about 40 mini bundt cakes.

Notes

Chocolate Chip Strawberry Bars

- 2 ½ c. flour
- 1 t. salt
- 1 t. baking soda
- 1 c. butter
- 2 c. brown sugar
- 2 eggs
- 3 c. oatmeal
- ¾ c. semi sweet chocolate chips
- ¾ c. strawberry preserves
- An additional ¾ c. semi sweet chocolate chips for the topping

Preheat oven to 350°.

Cream together butter, brown sugar and eggs. Sift together flour, salt, and baking soda. Add to the creamed mixture. Stir in oatmeal and chocolate chips. Press ¾ of the mixture into a 9"x13" pan. Reserve the remaining ¼ mixture. Spread the ¾ c. of strawberry preserves over the pressed mixture in pan. Crumble the reserved mixture on top of the strawberry mixture. Bake for 12-15 minutes or until done. Do not over-bake. Remove from the oven and sprinkle the ¾ c. of semi sweet chocolate chips on top of

Notes

Chocolate Chip Strawberry Bars Continued

the baked mixture while still hot. Place a cookie sheet over the pan to hold the heat in and melt the chocolate chips. Let sit for 10 minutes and then spread chocolate with a spatula. Refrigerate overnight and cut into bars. Makes about 24 bars depending on cut size.

Notes

Chocolate Crispy Cookies

- 2 ½ c. flour
- 1 t. baking powder
- 1 t. baking soda
- ½ t. salt
- 1 c. butter
- 1 c. sugar
- 1 c. brown sugar
- 2 eggs
- 2 t. vanilla
- 2 c. rice cereal (or Special K)
- 1 ½ c. coconut
- ½ c. raisins
- ½ c. golden raisins
- 1 ½ c. semi sweet chocolate chips
- ½ c. coconut – for sprinkling on top

Combine flour, baking powder, baking soda and salt in a small bowl. Set aside. In a medium bowl, beat butter until light and fluffy. Add the sugars, egg, and vanilla. Add the dry ingredients to the beaten mixture. Mix in the cereal, coconut, raisins, and chocolate chips. Drop by teaspoonful onto an ungreased cookie sheet. Lightly flatten each cookie with the bottom of a glass dipped in sugar. Top the cookie with a

Notes

Chocolate Crispy Cookies Continued

sprinkle of shredded coconut before baking. Bake in a 375° oven for 7-9 minutes or until lightly golden brown in color. Makes about 6 dozen tea cookies.

Notes

Crème Brule Tea Cookies

- 1 c. butter
- 1 c. powdered sugar
- 1 t. salt
- 2 T. Crème Brule loose tea – process in food processor until fine
- 1⅔ c. flour

Maple Glaze:

- 3¾ c. powdered sugar
- ½ c. maple syrup
- 1 t. maple extract
- Water to drizzling consistency
- Turbinado sugar

Cream butter and powdered sugar together. In a separate bowl mix together flour, salt, loose tea. Add to creamed mixture. Scoop out into cookies (about 1 teaspoon full). Flatten with a glass. Bake at 400° for 5 minutes. Cool completely and frost with Maple Glaze.

Maple Glaze:

Beat at low speed with electric mixer until smooth. Add more water if it's too thick.

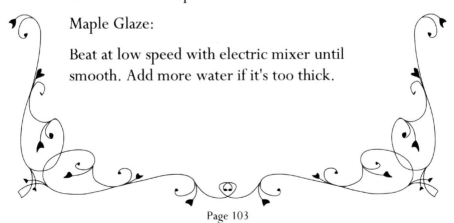

Notes

Crème Brule Tea Cookies
Continued

Drizzle on cookies and decorate with turbinado sugar. Let dry completely before storing.

Makes about 40 tea cookies.

Notes

Dena's Fabulous White Chocolate Orange Cup Cakes

These cupcakes are to die for! They are so moist and delicious! Experiment and add your own ingredients.

- 1 white cake mix with pudding in the mix
- 1¼ c. water
- ⅓ c. oil
- 3 egg whites
- Zest of 1 orange
- 1 t. orange juice
- ¼ c. real mayonnaise
- 1 c. white chocolate chips

Orange Cream Cheese Frosting:

- 3 pkg. (8oz) cream cheese, softened
- 1 T. orange juice
- 1 t. orange zest
- 4 c. powdered sugar

Preheat oven to 350°. Combine all ingredients in a large mixing bowl. Mix at medium speed for 3 minutes until well blended. Pour into mini cupcake pans lined with mini cupcake papers. Bake for 5-7 minutes or until done when a toothpick inserted comes out clean. Remove

Notes

Dena's Fabulous White Chocolate Orange Cup Cakes Continued

from pan and cool before frosting. Makes about 48 mini cupcakes (24 regular cupcake size-bake about 15-18 minutes).

Orange Cream Cheese Frosting:

In large bowl beat cream cheese, orange juice, zest until smooth. Gradually add powdered sugar to the mix 1 c. at a time. Continue beating until creamy and smooth in texture. Refrigerate until ready to use. Pipe onto the top of your cupcakes.

Notes

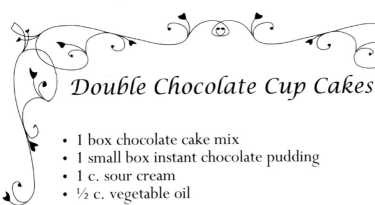

Double Chocolate Cup Cakes

- 1 box chocolate cake mix
- 1 small box instant chocolate pudding
- 1 c. sour cream
- ½ c. vegetable oil
- ½ c. water
- 4 eggs
- 1½ c. semi sweet chocolate chips

Chocolate Buttercream Frosting:

- ½ c solid shortening (the shortening sticks are wonderful)
- ½ c. butter, softened
- ¾ c. cocoa powder
- 1 t. vanilla extract
- 4 c. powdered sugar
- 3-4 T. milk

Preheat oven to 350°. Combine all cake ingredients in a large mixing bowl. Mix at medium speed for 3 minutes until well blended. Pour into mini cupcake pans lined with mini cupcake papers. Bake for 5-7 minutes or until done when a toothpick inserted comes out clean. Remove from pan and cool before frosting. Makes about 48 mini cupcakes (24 regular

Notes

Double Chocolate Cup Cakes Continued

cupcake size-bake about 15-18 minutes).

Chocolate Buttercream Frosting:

In large bowl cream shortening and butter with an electric mixer until light and fluffy. Add cocoa and vanilla. Mix well. Add powdered sugar one cup at a time. Icing will appear dry. Add milk and beat at medium speed until light and fluffy. Keep frosting covered with a damp cloth or paper towel until ready to use.

A fun decorative idea is to top the cupcake with marshmallows, chopped up chocolate bars and chopped walnuts to make "Rocky Road Cupcakes."

Notes

Double Chocolate Peppermint Bars

- 4 pkgs chocolate graham crackers (crushed)
- ¾ c. butter (melted)
- 1 c. semisweet chocolate chips
- 1 can sweetened condensed milk
- 1½ c. crushed peppermint candy
- ½ c. white chocolate chips

Process chocolate graham crackers in a food processor. Melt butter and mix well into graham cracker mixture with a fork. Press into the bottom of a 9"x13" baking pan. Sprinkle 1 c. of the crushed peppermint candy over the top of the graham cracker crust. Pour one can of the sweetened condensed milk over candy. Layer the white chocolate chips over the milk. Layer ½ c. of semi sweet chocolate chips. Layer the remaining peppermint candy and the rest of the semi sweet chocolate chips. Bake at 375° for 14 minutes. Remove from oven. While still hot, drizzle melted semi sweet chocolate chips over the top. Add another layer of melted white chocolate chips over the top. Sprinkle the top with more crushed peppermint candies. Cool and cut into bars. Makes about 24 bars depending on cut size.

Notes

Eggnog Tea Cakes

- 1 pkg. yellow cake mix
- 1 c. fresh eggnog
- ¼ c. oil
- 3 eggs
- 2 T. spiced rum
- ¼ t. ground nutmeg

Frosting:

- 1 8oz. pkg. cream cheese, softened
- 1 lb. powdered sugar
- 1½-3 t. eggnog
- 1 T. spiced rum
- Yellow food coloring (optional)

Preheat over to 350°. Spray mini bundt pans with flour cooking spray. In large mixing bowl, combine cake mix, eggnog, oil, eggs, rum and nutmeg. Beat at medium speed 3 minutes. Bake in mini bundt pans (12 in a pan) about 8-12 minutes or until done when a toothpick is inserted. Cool completely.

Frosting:

In a small bowl, beat cream cheese until fluffy.

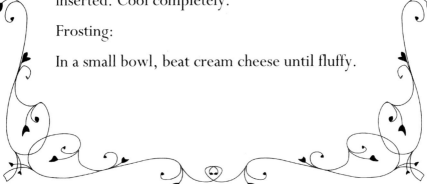

Notes

Eggnog Tea Cakes Continued

Gradually beat in powdered sugar. Add rum. Add eggnog a little at a time until desired consistency. Add food coloring if desired. We like to make the glaze thin enough so you can dip the cooled cakes into the glaze.

This recipe makes about 40 mini tea cakes.

Notes

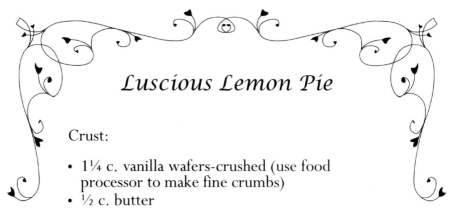

Luscious Lemon Pie

Crust:

- 1¼ c. vanilla wafers-crushed (use food processor to make fine crumbs)
- ½ c. butter

Filling:

- 1 can (14 oz) sweetened condensed milk
- ½ c. lemon juice
- 1 t. lemon peel or fresh zest
- 1 lemon – cut in ½ and use juice from ½
- 1 t. lemon extract
- 1 8 oz. container of whipped topping, thawed
- Whipping cream (optional – for garnish) – beat until stiff consistency

Crust:

Melt butter and mix in vanilla wafers. Press crumb mixture into a 9"x13" pan (sprayed with a non-stick spray.) Bake at 350° for 4-5 minutes. Cool.

Filling:

Beat sweetened condensed milk, lemon juice,

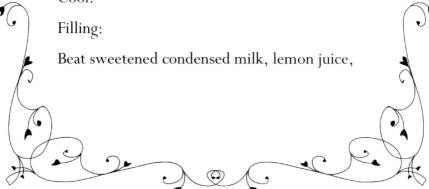

Notes

Luscious Lemon Pie
Continued

peel, ½ fresh squeezed lemon, and lemon extract in a small bowl until combined. Fold in whipped topping; pour into crust. Cover; refrigerate/freeze for 2 hours or until set. Cut into small squares. Place in small dishes, pipe on whipped cream, garnish with lemon slice.

Notes

Miniature Tea Party Cheesecakes

- 1 8oz. pkg. cream cheese, softened
- ¼ c. sugar
- 1½ t. lemon juice
- ½ t. grated lemon peel
- ¼ t. vanilla
- 1 egg

Crust:

- ⅓ c. graham cracker or vanilla wafer crumbs (process in food processor)
- 1 T. sugar
- 1 T. butter, melted

Topping:

- Cherry, strawberry, apricot preserves, or orange marmalade – your choice or a variety of each

Combine crumbs, sugar and butter. Press 1 t. crumb mixture onto bottom of paper-lined mini muffin cups.

Combine cream cheese, sugar, lemon juice, peel and vanilla, mixing at medium speed on mixer until well blended. Blend in egg; pour over crust, filling each cup ¾ full. Bake at 325° for

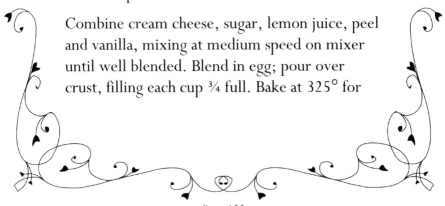

Notes

Miniature Tea Party Cheesecakes Continued

about 10-15 minnutes. Cool before removing from pan. Chill. Top with preserves just before serving. Makes about 12.

Notes

Patti's Pumpkin Muffins

- 1¾ c. flour
- ¼ t. baking powder
- 1 t. baking soda
- 1 t. salt
- ½ t. cinnamon
- ¼ t. ground cloves
- 1⅓ c. sugar
- ⅓ c. butter, softened
- 2 eggs
- 1 c. canned pumpkin
- ⅓ c. milk
- ½ t. vanilla
- ½-1 c. mini chocolate chips
- Nuts, raisins optional

Combine flour, baking powder, soda, salt, cinnamon and cloves. In another bowl, mix together sugar, butter and eggs. Add pumpkin, milk, and vanilla. Stir in dry ingredients. Add chocolate chips and optional ingredients.

Pour into desired pan-loaf pan or 12 cupcakes or 24 mini muffins. Bake at 350° until done. 55-60 min for loaf, 18-22 minutes for cupcakes, 10-15 for the mini muffins. Remember all ovens are

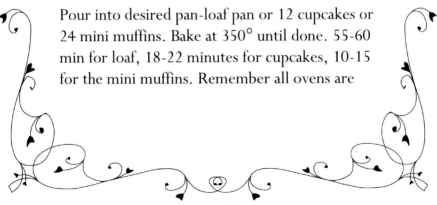

Notes

Patti's Pumpkin Muffins
Continued

different, so use a toothpick and test. When it comes out clean, it's done!

Patti says this is her no-fail recipe for those who don't cook. You can just mix everything in all at once and it still turns out. If you use more or less pumpkin they still turn out. You can make up the batter the night before and store in the refrigerator, then bake them the next morning, or even the morning after. One note however, she says they taste the best the day they are baked.

This recipe can be easily doubled or tripled.

Notes

Rum Balls

- 3 c. toasted pecans, walnuts, hazelnuts
- 2½ c. finely crushed vanilla wafers (use food processor to chop)
- 1 c. powdered sugar
- 4 T. cocoa powder
- 4 T. light corn syrup
- ½ c. spiced rum
- 1 c. powdered sugar saved for later use

Preheat oven to 350°. Place nuts on a cookie sheet and toast 5-8 minutes until lightly browned, do not over bake. Cool completely then chop finely.

Combine all ingredients together, mixing well. Chill for about 1 hour. Shape into 1 inch balls using a melon baller or small ice cream scoop. Roll balls in ½ c. powdered sugar. Store in an airtight container in the refrigerator. Serve at room temperature.

These taste better if made a few days ahead of time. They will keep about 2 weeks. You can reroll them in more powdered sugar if needed. Makes about 8 dozen balls.

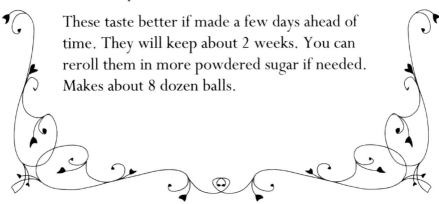

Notes

Toasted Coconut Tea Cakes

- 1 box yellow golden cake mix
- 1 lg. box "toasted coconut" instant pudding or "coconut cream" instant pudding
- 4 eggs
- ½ c. vegetable oil
- 1¼ c. water
- 1 t. coconut extract

Glaze:

- 4 oz cream cheese, softened
- ¼ c. canned coconut milk or whipping cream
- 1 box powdered sugar
- 1 t. coconut extract
- Toasted coconut for garnish (recipe follows)

Mix cake mix, pudding, oil, water and coconut extract together in a large mixing bowl. Gradually add eggs one at a time and mix 3 minutes on medium speed until well blended. Bake at 375° for 8-15 minutes until golden brown or when done when a toothpick is inserted. Cool completely.

Notes

Toasted Coconut Tea Cakes Continued

Glaze:

Mix all glaze ingredients together. Dip cooled cakes into glaze and top with toasted coconut. Makes about 40 mini bundt cakes. (Each bundt pan has 12 cakes on a pan).

To toast coconut:

Spread coconut on a cookie sheet. Toast at 375° for 5-6 minutes until lightly brown.

Notes

White Chocolate Cranberry Bars

- 4 c. crushed graham crackers
- ½ c. melted butter
- 2 c. shredded coconut
- 2 c. dried cranberries
- 1 c. walnuts, chopped
- 2 c. white chocolate chips
- 2 cans sweetened condensed milk

Topping:

- ½ c. mixture of white chocolate chips and chopped dried cranberries.

Combine crushed graham crackers and melted butter. Press mixture into the bottom of a 9"x13" pan. Layer with 1 c. coconut, 1 c. dried cranberries, ½ c. walnuts, and 1 c. white chocolate chips. Pour one can of sweetened condensed milk over the top of the ingredients. Repeat process: 1 c. coconut, 1 c. dried cranberries, ½ c. walnuts, and 1 c. white chocolate chips. Pour 1 can sweetened condensed milk over the top. Top with the combination of white chocolate chips and dried cranberries. Bake at 350° for about 18 minutes and browned lightly. Cool and then refrigerate until firm, preferably overnight. Cut into bars. Makes about 24-36 depending on the cut size.

Notes

Scones and Condiments

Tips on Making Scones

Use quality ingredients.

Use cold butter; don't let it soften. Cold butter makes the scones rise higher.

Drain fruit very well.

Add fruit last, barely mix it in to flour mixture.

Add only enough buttermilk to make dough stick together.

If dough is too sticky when you pat it on the floured board, add more flour.

If dough is too dry and crumbles when you try and pat it on the floured board, add more buttermilk.

If you are using frozen fruit, make sure it does not thaw out. Mix it in quickly and cut scones fast. If it thaws out, the dough is very sticky and a mess!

Make sure oven is hot and preheated to 400°.

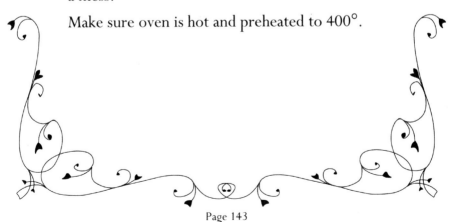

Blackberry Anniversary Scones

- 3 c. self-rising flour
- ½ c. granulated sugar
- ½ c. blackberries
- ¼ c. white chocolate chips
- 1 stick of unsalted butter
- ½ to ¾ c. buttermilk

Mix together flour and sugar. Use pastry cutter to cut in butter. Mixture should resemble coarse cornmeal. Add chocolate chips and gently fold in blackberries. Add enough of the buttermilk to make the mixture come together. If mixture is too dry add more buttermilk until it barely holds together. Turn out on a floured board. Pat out to 1" thick. Cut with a small biscuit cutter or into triangles. Bake in preheated 400° oven for 12-20 minutes, or until nicely browned and done-depending on your oven. Glaze when cool. Scones can be stored in a sealed container and reheated in foil. Makes about 15 scones.

Glaze (optional as these are pretty sweet without glaze)

Mix together 1 c. powdered sugar and 2-3 T. milk until the desired consistency. Dip scones in glaze. Let set.

Notes

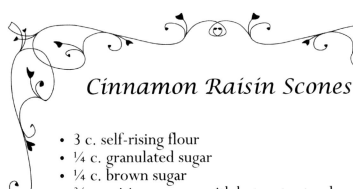

Cinnamon Raisin Scones

- 3 c. self-rising flour
- ¼ c. granulated sugar
- ¼ c. brown sugar
- ¾ c. raisins – cover with hot water to plump them up, let sit 5 minutes, drain completely
- 1 T. cinnamon
- 1 stick of unsalted butter
- ½ to ¾ c. buttermilk

Glaze:

- 1 8 oz pkg cream cheese
- 1 lb. box powdered sugar
- 1 t. vanilla
- 2 t. or more of milk

Mix together flour, granulated sugar and cinnamon. Use pastry cutter to cut in butter. Mixture should resemble coarse cornmeal. Add raisins. Fold in brown sugar. Add enough of the buttermilk to make the mixture come together. If mixture is too dry add more buttermilk until it barely holds together. Turn out on a floured board. Pat out to 1 inch thick. Cut with a small biscuit cutter or into triangles. Bake in preheated 400° oven for 12-20 minutes, or until

Notes

Cinnamon Raisin Scones
Continued

nicely browned and done-depending on your oven. Glaze when cool. Scones can be stored in a sealed container and reheated in foil. Makes about 15 scones.

For the glaze, blend cream cheese and powdered sugar together. Add vanilla. Add 2 t. milk or more until desired consistency. If you make the glaze thin enough you can dip the scones in glaze. Let set.

Notes

Mandarin Orange Scones

- 3 c. self-rising flour
- ½ c. granulated sugar
- Zest of one orange
- ¼ c. mandarin oranges pureed in food processor
- ¼ c. mandarin orange segments, cut in half
- 1 stick of unsalted butter
- ½ to ¾ c. buttermilk

Glaze:

- 1 c. powdered sugar
- 2-3 T. mandarin orange juice

Mix together flour and sugar. Use pastry cutter to cut in butter. Mixture should resemble coarse cornmeal. Add zest, pureed mandarins and mandarin segments. Add enough of the buttermilk to make the mixture come together. If mixture is too dry add more buttermilk until it barely holds together. Turn out on a floured board. Pat out to 1 inch thick. Cut with a small biscuit cutter or into triangles. Bake in preheated 400° oven for 12-20 minutes, or until nicely browned and done-depending on your oven. Glaze when cool. Scones can be stored in

Notes

Mandarin Orange Scones
Continued

a sealed container and reheated in foil. Makes about 15 scones.

Glaze:

Mix together 1 c. powdered sugar and 2-3 T. mandarin orange juice until the desired consistency. Dip scones in glaze. Let set.

Notes

Raspberry Chocolate Scones

- 3 c. self-rising flour
- ½ c. granulated sugar
- ½ c. raspberries, washed and well drained
- ¼ c. semisweet chocolate chips
- 1 stick of unsalted butter
- ½-¾ c. buttermilk

Mix together flour and sugar. Use pastry cutter to cut in butter. Mixture should resemble coarse cornmeal. Add chocolate chips and very gently fold in raspberries. Add enough of the buttermilk to make the mixture come together. If mixture is too dry add more buttermilk until it barely holds together. Turn out on a floured board. Pat out to 1" thick. Cut with a small biscuit cutter or into triangles. Bake in preheated 400° oven for 12-20 minutes, or until nicely browned and done-depending on your oven. Glaze when cool. Scones can be stored in a sealed container and reheated in foil. Makes about 15 scones.

Glaze (optional as these are pretty sweet without glaze).

Notes

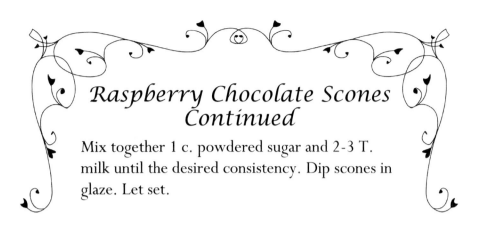

Raspberry Chocolate Scones
Continued

Mix together 1 c. powdered sugar and 2-3 T. milk until the desired consistency. Dip scones in glaze. Let set.

Notes

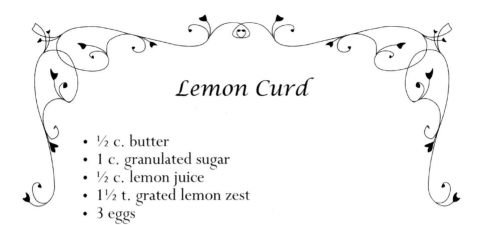

Lemon Curd

- ½ c. butter
- 1 c. granulated sugar
- ½ c. lemon juice
- 1½ t. grated lemon zest
- 3 eggs

Melt butter in microwave for 1 minute. Beat eggs in a glass bowl with an electric mixer until frothy. Mix in butter, sugar, lemon juice and zest. Microwave on HIGH for 3 minutes.

Beat mixture again until smooth. Microwave on HIGH for another 3 minutes. Beat mixture again until smooth. Refrigerate until set/cool. Lemon curd will keep up to 2 weeks in refrigerator.

Makes about 1 cup of lemon curd.

Notes

Devonshire Cream

This is not a "true" Devonshire cream, but our customers love our version.

- 1 8 oz. pkg. cream cheese, softened
- 2 c. powdered sugar
- ½ freshly squeezed lemon
- 2 t. vanilla
- 1 c. sour cream

In a small bowl with an electric mixer, beat cream cheese, lemon juice, and vanilla. Gradually beat in powdered sugar. Fold in sour cream.

Makes 1½ cups.

Notes

Index

Index Continued

Index Continued

About the Author

Amy Lawrence began her tea room in August of 2003. Previously she had been a special education teacher for 11 years teaching learning disabled and autistic students. She took a two year break to be home with her two sons. In August of 2002 while having tea with my mother, she said, "This is what I want to do now! I want my own tea room. I love to cook and have always enjoyed catering for special parties." In November of 2002, she attended a tea conference and also became a certified tea consultant. It all began from there. With the help of dedicated family and friends, she finally opened her tea room on August 27, 2003. In July 2006, Tea Experience Digest named An Afternoon to Remember Tea Parlor and Gifts the Reader's Choice Award for Best Small City Tea Room in the U.S. At the present time, Amy has self-published 5 cookbooks and is currently working on a new book on afternoon teas.

CPSIA information can be obtained at www.ICGtesting.com
Printed in the USA
BVOW04s1944280414

351674BV00001B/8/P